PIONEER VALLEY

MICHELLE KWAN

KATHERINE RAWSON

TABLE OF CONTENTS

A Young Skater 2
School for Michelle 6
Going for the Gold 8
Michelle Today 16
Timeline 20

A YOUNG SKATER

Michelle Kwan was born in California in 1980. She started skating when she was just five years old. She became one of the best figure skaters in the world.

Michelle worked hard
to become a good skater.
She wanted to skate
in the Olympics.
She skated every day.
Michelle skated before school,
and she skated after school.

SCHOOL FOR MICHELLE

When Michelle was ten years old, she went to a special skating school. It was called Ice Castle.

When Michelle
was 13 years old,
she stopped going
to public school.
She was too busy skating.
She had help
from special teachers
called tutors.

When Michelle was 16 years old, she won the World Championships.

When Michelle was 18 years old, she got to skate in the Olympics. She was so happy to win a silver medal!

When Michelle
was 22 years old,
she got to skate
in the Olympics again.
Michelle fell on the ice,
but she got up
and kept on skating.
This time, Michelle
won the bronze medal.

When Michelle
was 26 years old,
she went to the Olympics
one more time.
This time, she hurt her leg,
and she did not get to skate.
This was Michelle's last Olympics.

MICHELLE TODAY

Now, Michelle talks to people about playing sports and staying healthy.

▶ Michelle works with the President and first lady, Michelle Obama, and a group called the President's Council on Fitness, Sports, and Nutrition.

In 2012, Michelle's name was added to the U.S. Figure Skating Hall of Fame and the World Figure Skating Hall of Fame.

Michelle doesn't skate
in competitions anymore.
She still has many fans.
People remember
how hard she worked
and how she never gave up.

TIMELINE

1980 Born in California on July 7

1985 Begins skating at age five

1996 Wins first of five gold medals at World Skating Championship

1998 Wins Silver Olympic medal

2002 Wins Bronze Olympic medal

2006 Named as a public diplomacy ambassador

2009 Graduates from University of Denver

2012 Inducted into the United States Figuring Skating Hall of Fame